# Breath for the Breathless

# Breath for the Breathless

## Liturgy for Life's Difficult Seasons

GLORY CUMBOW

RESOURCE *Publications* • Eugene, Oregon

BREATH FOR THE BREATHLESS
Liturgy for Life's Difficult Seasons

Copyright © 2020 Glory Cumbow. All rights reserved. Except for brief quotations in critical publications or reviews, no part of this book may be reproduced in any manner without prior written permission from the publisher. Write: Permissions, Wipf and Stock Publishers, 199 W. 8th Ave., Suite 3, Eugene, OR 97401.

Resource Publications
An Imprint of Wipf and Stock Publishers
199 W. 8th Ave., Suite 3
Eugene, OR 97401

www.wipfandstock.com

PAPERBACK ISBN: 978-1-7252-7979-7
HARDCOVER ISBN: 978-1-7252-7978-0
EBOOK ISBN: 978-1-7252-7980-3

Manufactured in the U.S.A. 09/10/20

# Contents

| | | |
|---|---|---|
| | Introduction | 1 |
| 1 | Mass Tragedy | 3 |
| 2 | Mental Health and Suicide | 8 |
| 3 | Blue Christmas or Longest Night | 17 |
| 4 | Child Loss, Miscarriage, Infertility, and Parenthood | 21 |
| 5 | LGBTQIA+ Remembrance | 29 |
| 6 | Denouncing Racism | 35 |
| 7 | Closing a Church | 42 |
| 8 | Liturgy for Various Circumstances | 48 |
| 9 | Praying with Youth | 59 |
| 10 | Praying with Children | 68 |

# Introduction

CLERGY ARE OFTEN ON the frontlines when tragedy strikes, when people face trauma, and when a community is wounded. This is when pastoral care instincts kick in and we offer care. Holding a space with the freedom to cry, to pray, to hold one another, to share stories, and to just be together is an essential function of the church. While having these spaces with no agenda but to be present is an important ministry of the church, there may come a moment when the community turns to the pastor for a specific source of comfort, for closure, for a ritual.

It's likely that the spiritual leaders are shocked and grieving themselves during these trying times. Creating liturgy may be the last thing they would want to focus their energy on. Often, there are not widely accessible resources that a pastor can turn to when disaster forays into our lives, and that leaves the individual scrambling to piece something together. Many of the available resources are for general purposes, and sometimes the words to fit a specific circumstance are nowhere to be found. I have seen other clergy reaching out in emergencies, anxiously asking for prayers or litanies that others have used in these situations. These conversations sparked the idea for this resource.

When we need ritual to put some form of order to the chaos, I hope pastors will reach for this liturgical book on the shelf and be ready to go in a pinch. This book offers liturgy for the specific experiences of mass tragedy, mental illness, child loss, LGBTQIA+

communal remembrances, and other circumstances when the church needs to put words to the pain that the people are feeling. When a community finds the wind knocked out of them, I hope that these words open their hearts to God's life-giving breath as they find their footing to move forward. These words will not be a fix for pain and suffering, but they may be a start on the path to healing. May this book provide the steadiness to breathe again as you navigate the pain of your community together, seeking God's comfort.

With hope in the resurrected Christ,
*Glory Cumbow*

# 1

# Mass Tragedy

HURRICANES AND EARTHQUAKES LEAVE homes in shambles. All too often, we hear of an active shooter in a school or a business. Terrorists drive cars through public gatherings, targeting people walking on sidewalks. We live in a violent and dangerous world, and we are often caught off guard when casualty numbers skyrocket. Churches often mobilize to help those in need, offering their facilities to help those who have been displaced, raising funds, distributing food, and advocating for those who have been hurt and oppressed. It is always an inspiration to see God at work in the community through the church. Once needs have begun to be met, people often want to gather. They need comfort, hope, a place to put their confusion and anger, and often they look to clergy for this outlet. This is when it would be appropriate to offer a worship service for the community who is seeking for some stability after such chaos. I offer this liturgy for natural disasters, for communities rocked by gun violence, for communities ravaged by attacks and warfare, and for all mass tragedies our people face. I also offer a prayer for an individual who may be experiencing survivor's guilt to be used in private pastoral care circumstances. When dozens, hundreds, and thousands of people find themselves grieving, displaced, and at a loss, may these words provide guidance.

Breath for the Breathless

## WORSHIP SERVICE

Call to Worship (from Lamentations 3)
  Leader: Oh Lord, see our distress.
  **People: Our hearts, our minds, our stomachs churn.**
  Leader: Our spirits are wrung.
  **People: We are groaning in this time of trouble.**
  Leader: Who will comfort us?
  **All: Come, Lord Jesus, come.**

Hymn

Call to Confession
As we address the darkness in the world, let us not neglect the darkness in our own hearts. We are in need of an outpouring of healing, so let the healing begin in us. Let us confess our sins to God and one another.

Confession
**God of peace, you have shown us that the way to a loving world is through peacemaking. You have revealed to us that peacemaking relies on creating a supportive, merciful, and just community. We confess that we often focus on our own pain, forgetting that healing comes from sharing our burdens with one another. Empower us to resist being self-focused, so that we might reach out to our neighbors to share our journey of grief together. Embolden us to be communities of peace that persist against the destructive chaos around us. We ask this in the confidence of your mercy through Christ. Amen.**
(Silence.)

Assurance of Pardon
Beloved, there is good news for those who crave the light amidst the darkness. Jesus is in the business of healing, forgiving, and making all things new. This gift is offered to each and every one of us. In the name of Jesus Christ, we are forgiven. Amen.

Prayer of Illumination

## Mass Tragedy

Speak, oh Lord. We yearn to hear your voice. Send forth your Holy Spirit to revive us. Amen.

Scripture Suggestions
Isaiah 53:3–9; Lamentations 3:1–3, 22–25; John 1:1–5; 1 Peter 2:21–25

Sermon
*A sermon may be offered that directly references the tragedy at hand. Hearing scripture applied to the specific circumstance will be necessary for the community as they are longing for the Good News. Sometimes tragedies are briefly mentioned in worship services but as a side note. A sermon reflecting on the rawness of a disaster or tragedy may exactly meet the community's need.*

Hymn

Affirmation of Faith (from Philippians 2)
We believe that God is all-powerful and all-loving. This is shown to us through God's Son, Jesus, who came to earth in human likeness. God exalts the name of Jesus on high, and we believe that Jesus is Lord. Jesus did not exploit his equality with God but became a servant. Jesus humbled himself to the point of death on the cross. We believe in the Holy Spirit who shares in love, compassion, and sympathy. It is in Christ we share the same mind and the same Spirit so that we may love one another. Together we glorify the Holy Trinity, who suffer alongside us, sharing in love.

Prayer of the People

Option A
Creator God, we praise you for the ground we stand upon and for grounding us in your steadfast love. When the earth beneath us and the world around us stirs, we are cast into fear, grief, and anger. We have lost our homes and our belongings to *(name tragedy here, i.e.: earthquake, hurricane X, tsunami, etc.)* When we stand among the rubble of tragedy we toss our hands up in the air, broken and exasperated, looking for some sense in the chaos. Where are you, God? Why has this happened? Come, Lord, come! Loving God, hear our cries. Be gracious to us as we come to you with honesty

and raw emotions. Please whisper healing in the silence and hold us fast when we fall down too exhausted to carry on.

Faithful God, we ask *(here you may add specific prayer petitions and requests, e.g.: "We ask that you console the families in the flood zone whose homes are in standing water from hurricane X, and help us as we shelter and feed them.")* We especially pray for those who have lost loved ones to *(name tragedy here.)* We are mourning them, and we are stretched to our limits. We have lost so much, and we desperately need your strength to carry on. Oh God, please enter into our pain, weeping with us and comforting us. Walk with us on this journey of grief and restoration. Rebuild our hope as we rebuild our communities. We ask all of these things with confidence in your divine mercy and in the name of your Son, Jesus Christ. Amen.

Option B

Jesus Christ, God-with-us, we are grateful that you are the one who stands with us in the face of violence. You know firsthand the agony of being a victim of public, unjust rage. You know what it's like to be torn apart by the hands of wrath. From our own tatters, we cry out to our wounded Savior, whose wounds heal. We are angry and we are hurting because of *(name tragedy here, i.e.: the shooting, the terrorist attack, the bombing, etc.)* We mourn the loss of our loved ones, and in our anger we cry out for justice!

Hold those who desire bloodshed accountable for their violent ways. Help us always to speak out against those who seek to steal, kill, and destroy. Jesus, our Savior, you have shown us the way to overcome violence and evil. You've revealed that peacemaking is the way to a reconciled world. Embolden us to be the peacemakers who hunger and thirst after righteousness and treat our fellow humans with dignity and respect.

As we huddle together in our distress, wrap your arms around us. Use the hands that were once nailed to the cross to reach out and hold ours. May your embrace spark the hope that you have overcome the powers of death, and that injustice and violence do not have the final word. It is in your name we ask these things. Amen.

The Lord's Prayer

Hymn

Benediction
May the God of mercy embrace you with comfort and peace,
May the Christ of the resurrection help you face down death and darkness,
May the Spirit who gives life help you catch your breath. Amen.

Suggested Hymns
> "God Weeps with Us Who Weep and Mourn"; Author: Thomas H. Troeger; Composer: Sally Ann Morris
>
> "Goodness is Stronger than Evil"; Author: Desmond Tutu; Composer: John L. Bell
>
> "I Want Jesus to Walk with Me"; Arranger: Nolan Williams, Jr.; Composer: Unknown
>
> "Precious Lord, Take My Hand"; Author and Arranger: Thomas A. Dorsey; Composer: George N. Allen

## Prayer for someone experiencing survivor's guilt

Source of life, God you are the author of the world and our lives. We praise you for your sovereignty. God, we do not understand why such terrible situations befall us. We do not understand the horror of this world, and we feel the weight of life and death. As we struggle to make sense of the tragedy of this world, sometimes we feel guilty for surviving when others around us have died. We wonder why we are here, and they are not. As we ask these questions and feel this weight, we pray for *(name)* and the guilt they are feeling. Please ease their pain and guilt and remind them of their value and purpose. We are grateful that *(name)* is here with us today; their life is a testament to goodness and hope amidst tragedy. *(Name's)* life is a gift to us all. Help us as we go forward and mourn those who've passed away. Their lives were a gift too, and we are so grateful for the time we had them. Help us to support *(name)* as the Body of Christ. We ask these things in Jesus' name. Amen.

# 2

# Mental Health and Suicide

THE CONVERSATION ABOUT MENTAL health and suicide is growing as our society gains more compassion and understanding. Depression, anxiety, post-traumatic stress disorder (PTSD), bipolar disorder, schizophrenia, and other forms of mental illness are not signs of weakness or evidence of a poor spiritual life but are treatable conditions that many people, including pastors, live with each day. In an attempt to destigmatize mental illness, many people speak about mental health in a positive way. Therapy and medication are effective treatments and are becoming widely encouraged for anyone who needs them.

Suicide is a painful experience for those left in its wake. This specific grief of losing someone who has died by suicide sometimes causes guilt or the urge to place blame. Suicide needs to be discussed in our churches, not hushed in shame and blame. Talking about grief openly can allow the community to come together and find healing in one another. Speaking freely and positively about mental health resources can help someone who may feel like there is no other way out.

I offer this liturgy as a way to talk about mental health and grieve the effects of suicide. The service for mental health can be used for communal worship during Mental Health Awareness

## MENTAL HEALTH AND SUICIDE

Month in May. The service for suicide remembrance can be used during Suicide Prevention Month in September. There are also prayers for someone who has survived a suicide attempt and someone struggling with self-harm. May these words provide light.

## WORSHIP SERVICE FOR MENTAL HEALTH

Call to Worship (From Jonah 2)
  Leader: I called out to the Lord in my distress.
  **People: I was cast in the deep, the waves and the billows surrounded me.**
  Leader: I was sinking down, my life was ebbing away.
  **People: I remembered you, Oh Lord, and I prayed to you.**
  Leader: You brought me up from the pit.
  **All: Deliverance belongs to the Lord.**

Hymn

Call to Confession
Healing begins with laying down all the guilt and shame we carry. The burden is too heavy, and our merciful God is willing to liberate us. Let us confess our sins to God, with confidence in God's steadfast love.

Confession
**Oh God, you are loving and merciful. You show us unconditional love, even when we feel unworthy. We confess that we often see ourselves through the lens of self-loathing. We are hard on ourselves, picking out the things we dislike and focusing on every flaw. Forgive us for when we do not love ourselves. Reveal your image created in us. Help us to love ourselves, so that we can love you and love others better. Embolden us to embrace who you have created us to be. We ask this in the name of Jesus Christ. Amen.**

*(Silence.)*

Assurance of Pardon
Fear not! You are loved and precious in God's sight. In Christ, God knows the depths of human pain and seeks to bring healing. It is also in Christ we are forgiven. Amen.

Prayer of Illumination
Holy Spirit, our hearts long for your presence, our ears tingle for a good word. Satisfy our hearts' desire to have some hope from hearing the Good News of Jesus Christ. Amen.

Scripture Suggestions
1 Kings 19:1–8; Psalm 46:1–3; Matthew 8:1–4, 14–17; Colossians 1:11–14

Homily
*Here a brief reflection on the Scriptures may be offered. This is a powerful opportunity for Scripture to be used to break the stigma surrounding mental health. For those who have carried shame and silence surrounding their mental health struggle, speaking aloud this pain from the pulpit can truly empower the congregation.*

Hymn

Affirmation of Faith (from Mark 4)
We believe in the peace of Jesus Christ. When the storm raged and the followers of Christ panicked, Jesus was at peace. When the boat that carried Jesus and the disciples was swamped with water, Jesus was at peace. When Jesus awoke and commanded the storm to be still, Jesus was at peace. We believe that the wind and the sea obey him at his word. We believe that Jesus stands by us in fear and distress, calming the storms that rage around us. We believe in the peace of Jesus Christ.

Prayer of the People
Oh Lord, you fill the hungry with good things. We are grateful that you are the source of living waters. We are starved for love. We are parched for peace. Our hands are reaching out to you. Meet us here. Fill us with what we crave. Hold onto us and don't let go.
*(Silence.)*

## Mental Health and Suicide

Oh God, who makes all things right and puts everything in order, bring calm. When our thoughts race, when our anxieties paralyze us, when our spirits fall into despair, when our minds feel out of control, please cease the chaos.
*(Silence.)*
Creator who breathes the breath of life, reinvigorate us. Our daily life, our stress, our traumas, our memories, they threaten to choke the life out of us. The weight of the world shatters our bones and takes our breath. Life-giver, sustain the life you've given us.
*(Silence.)*
God almighty, sometimes it's too much, it's too much, it's too much. You are strong, and we turn these troubles over into your power. Carry our burdens and carry us. We ask these things in the name of your Son. Amen.

The Lord's Prayer

Anointing and Laying on of Hands
*The pastor or presider may come down from the chancel and stand before the congregation to invite all who would like to be anointed and prayed over to come forward. If a kneeling bench is available, those who come forward may kneel; standing before the pastor or presider is also appropriate. Each individual may make their request known for prayer, and the pastor or presider can anoint their forehead with oil with the sign of the cross and lay hands on them to pray. Some individuals may have an aversion to touch, as it may trigger the person depending upon their mental health circumstances. If accommodations need to be made for the physical aspects of this portion of the service, one can be anointed on the palm of the hand or opt-out of the anointing and simply ask for a blessing. For the laying on of hands, the pastor or presider can lay their hands on the head or shoulder. If the individual has an aversion to touch, the pastor or presider may simply hold their hands out to pray over the person. A hymn may be sung or soft music may play.*

Anointing Prayer
As I anoint you with oil, may you be filled with the peace of God, the healing of Christ, and the power of the Holy Spirit. **Amen.**

Laying on of Hands Prayer or Blessing
Holy Spirit, come down and fill your child with peace and healing for wholeness. Speak power and life over them to face each battle and challenge with strength. May your beloved child be sustained, fed, and cared for by your presence and those you send into their life. **Amen.**

Hymn

Benediction
May the Creator of the universe remind you of your value,
May the Savior of the world bring healing to your whole being,
May the Sustaining Spirit pour out the peace that passes all understanding,
Today and every day, now and forever. Amen.

Suggested Hymns
"Be Still, My Soul"; Author: Katharina von Schlegel; Translator: Jane Laurie Borthwick; Composer: Jean Sibelius
"Dona Nobis Pacem"; Author: Latin Prose; Composer: Unknown; Arranger: Eric T. Myers
"I Need Thee Every Hour"; Author: Annie S. Hawks; Refrain Author and Composer: Robert Lowry
"Spirit of the Living God"; Author and Composer: Daniel Iverson

## WORSHIP SERVICE FOR SUICIDE REMEMBRANCE

*As people enter for worship, provide each one a flower to be used for the act of remembrance. Have the Christ candle lit on a table near the pulpit at the beginning of the service.*

Call to Worship (from Matthew 11 and Luke 23)
   Leader: Jesus said, "Come to me, all who are weary, and I will give you rest."
   **People: "I am gentle and humble in heart, and you will find rest for your souls."**

## Mental Health and Suicide

Leader: The criminal on the cross said, "Remember me when you come into your kingdom."
People: Jesus said, "Today you will be with me in Paradise."
Leader: Jesus invites us to bring our burdens to him;
People: He feels our pain, he suffers with us.
All: We have hope that Jesus remembers us in his kingdom.

Hymn

Prayer of Illumination
We need you, Holy Spirit. Reveal to us the power of Jesus who is the resurrection and the life. Through the spoken Word, give us peace. Amen.

Scripture Suggestions
Job 28:12–15, 24–28; Psalm 34:15–19; John 1:1–5; Romans 8:35–39

Homily
*A brief reflection on the Scriptures in the form of a homily may be proclaimed. There is often blame, shame, and fear surrounding the death of someone who has died by suicide. This can be an opportunity to alleviate some of the pain and stigma through proclamation of Scripture.*

A Time of Sharing and Testimony
*At this time those in attendance can share about a loved one who has died by suicide.*

Hymn

Affirmation of Faith (from Revelation 21)
We believe that God is coming to bring a new heaven and a new earth. The old will pass away and the new will come. God will live with us, making God's own home with humankind. We believe that death will be no more, and God will wipe every tear from our eyes. There will be no more mourning, and our pain will end. We believe that God is the Alpha and the Omega, the beginning and the end. God provides the water of life to all who are thirsty. God

is coming to make all things new, and all the evil that causes our suffering will be destroyed. Praise be to God.

Acts of Remembrance
*An arrangement of "Dona Nobis Pacem" can be played during this time. The congregation can come forward and lay their flower on the table in front of the Christ candle in remembrance of a loved one or as a prayer for those who experience suicidal thoughts.*

Prayer of the People
Gracious God, you are an ever-flowing fountain of grace. You hear our prayers, you have compassion for our suffering, and you hold us as we grieve. Reassure us that it is okay not to be okay all the time. Thank you for being our stronghold when we are weak and weary from the forces around us. Please be with us now, reminding us that you never abandon us in our pain and distress. Strengthen us in the silence.
*(Silence.)*
Loving God, as you draw us into your peace as we hurt, hear our cries to you. We miss our loved ones who have died by suicide. We don't understand why this has happened to us, and to them. Some of us even blame ourselves, carrying shame and regret. Help us to know it's not our fault. Show us how to let go of these feelings that continue to wound us. Soothe our heartache in the silence.
*(Silence.)*
Precious Lord, help us to trust in your eternal love. In life and death, we belong to you. Comfort the hearts who fear that suicide has separated our loved ones not only from us, but also from you. Ensure us that nothing, not even death, can separate us from your love. As we cling to you and hold tight to your presence, help us to rest in the assurance that your arms are wide enough to carry us and the beloved people we miss so dearly. Hold us close in the silence.
*(Silence.)*

The Lord's Prayer

Hymn

# Mental Health and Suicide

Benediction
The Lord be with your Spirit, and grace be with you,
In the name of the Father, Son, and the Holy Spirit. Amen.

Suggested Hymns
    "God Be the Love to Search and Keep Me (Oh Christ, Surround Me)"; Author and Composer: Richard Bruxvoort Colligan
    "Jesus, Remember Me"; Author: Taizé Community; Composer: Jacques Berthier
    "Lord, Listen to Your Children Praying"; Author and Composer: Ken Medema
    "Swing Low, Sweet Chariot"; Author and Composer: Traditional African-American Spiritual; Arranger: Robert Nathaniel Dett

## Prayer for someone who has survived a suicide attempt

Creator God who crafted the stars in the sky, we give you thanks for small beacons that break up the void of darkness. The void sometimes calls to us, draws us in to oppress us, to crush us, to suck the air out of our lungs. Oh Lord, sometimes it is just too much! We ask that you give us a spark here, a twinkle there, some form of hope and light that we can run to, hold in our hands, and carry on our way. We need something to grasp onto tightly to keep us holding on to the next breath, to the next day. God, surround your child *(name)* here and now with the peace that passes all understanding. Provide them with support from each moment to the next, knowing that they are loved and worthy. Thank you for creating *(name)*. We are so glad that they are here with us. Pour out your Spirit of healing and let us gather as a family to hold each other up and to be the sparks of hope for one another. In the name of Jesus Christ who has faced down the void and faces it with us now. Amen.

## Prayer for someone struggling with self-harm

God of sweet peace and tender love, you softly call us to a life of wholeness. Thank you for your caring Spirit. This world that we live in often opposes all things gentle and kind. Evil rages against the goodness and the abundant life you wish for us. Sometimes the darkness that encompasses us becomes too much to bear, causing our hearts to hurt which can manifest physically. Please, God, speak words of life to your child *(name.)* Let them know how valuable they are to us, and how important their voice, talents, hopes, and dreams are. Banish the voices that lie to *(name)* and tell them that they are unworthy of love and happiness. *(Name)* is worthy of every happiness. Help us, your church, to reassure them of their importance to the body of Christ. Let goodness reign so that self-harm may end and self-love will begin. In the name of Jesus, who shares the pain of scars. Amen.

# 3

# Blue Christmas or Longest Night

THE HOLIDAYS AREN'T EASY and joyful for everyone. While many people enjoy family gatherings, gifts, feasts, vacations, and a sense of happiness, others struggle with mental and physical illness, grief, family estrangement, unemployment, homelessness, or other painful experiences. Often people are expected to feign happiness so as not to bring others down. A Blue Christmas or Longest Night service is an opportunity for the church to recognize the suffering people experience around the holidays. It generally happens just before Christmas, often on December 21 which is the winter solstice or the longest night of the year. Since this worship service offers the unique challenge of being somber during a normally anticipatory and joyful time, clergy have sometimes found themselves at a loss for creating such a service. I offer this liturgy as a template for clergy and an outlet for the pain felt by the community. May these words provide peace.

## WORSHIP SERVICE

*For the act of remembrance, the congregation members will each need a candle to hold. As people enter the sanctuary, have candles in baskets for everyone to take one.*

## Breath for the Breathless

Call to Worship (From Psalm 61)
Leader: Hear my cry, Oh God. Listen to my prayer.
**People: From the end of the earth I call to you when my heart is faint.**
Leader: Lead me to the rock that is higher than I,
**People: For you are my refuge, a strong tower against all evil.**
Leader: Let me abide with you forever,
**All: Let me take shelter under your wings.**

Hymn
*During this time an acolyte or an usher can bring in the light for the Advent candles.*

Call to Confession
Our God is the source of all mercy, overflowing with healing for our souls. Let us enter into the rivers of mercy so that we might be washed clean.

Confession
**God of grace, we are grateful that you love all that we are. We bring our broken hearts to you, trusting your mercy to forgive the mistakes of our past, renew our spirits in the present, and guide our steps into the future. Our world needs your healing poured out over the nations, so let this work begin in us. Amen.**
*(Silence.)*

Assurance of Pardon
Beloved, rest assured that the Christ who is the Word made flesh knows the depths of pain and brokenness. The same Jesus who had a humble birth and died on the cross, also resurrected and told all of his friends to tell of this good news. In the name of Jesus Christ, we are forgiven. Amen.

Prayer of Illumination
Holy Spirit, make your presence known to us. Whisper your word to us as we sit in silence, craving a message from you. Quiet the noise around us and sit with us in this moment. Amen.

# Blue Christmas or Longest Night

Scripture Suggestions
Psalm 42:1–5; Isaiah 40:1–8; Luke 14:15–24; 1 John 1:5–7

Homily or Testimonies
*A brief reflection on the Scriptures in the form of a homily may be proclaimed, or this time could be offered as a time of testimony for those in attendance.*

Hymn

Affirmation of Faith (from Matthew 5)
We believe that Jesus blesses those who are hurting, who are seeking, and who are sharing kindness in the world. The kingdom of heaven belongs to the poor in spirit. Those who mourn will be comforted. The meek will inherit the earth. Those who hunger and thirst for righteousness will be filled. The merciful will receive mercy. Those with pure hearts will see God. Peacemakers will be called the children of God. The kingdom of heaven belongs to those who are persecuted. We believe that Jesus sees us, hears us, and welcomes us into the kingdom. Praise to our Lord and Savior, Jesus Christ.

Acts of Remembrance
*This is a time to recognize the pain and suffering of those in the service. At this time the congregation can sing a "Kyrie" or "Dona Nobis Pacem." Invite all who would like to come forward to light a candle of their own, taking light from the Advent wreath. The candle can be a remembrance of someone they love, a sign of something they are struggling with, a symbol of hope, a prayer for healing, or any other symbol they would like to hold a light for.*

Prayer of the People
Christ who entered the pain of our world, we call out for your mercy. You came in flesh and you know the sufferings of this life. You knew the pain of loss as you wept over Lazarus. Please, have mercy for the hearts that grieve over lost loved ones.
    **Lord have mercy. Christ have mercy.**
    Christ, you know how it feels to be abandoned; all of your disciples fled as you were arrested. You know how it feels to be

betrayed by one of your closest friends. Please, have mercy on all of those who are feeling alone, abandoned, and excluded.
**Lord have mercy. Christ have mercy.**
Jesus, we know that you have compassion for the sick. Instead of backing away from those who were ill and unclean, you reached out and healed them. Please, have mercy on all who are fighting physical, mental, emotional, and spiritual battles.
**Lord have mercy. Christ have mercy.**
Lord and Savior, you know what it means to be hurt, to be physically abused. You know what it means to be wounded by the hands of others. You were treated with injustice by the powers of the government; you have been a refugee; you have been wrongfully imprisoned. Please, have mercy on all who have been abused and those who have suffered injustice.
**Lord have mercy. Christ have mercy.**
*(Silence.)*

The Lord's Prayer

Hymn

Benediction
May Jesus, born in the filth of a stable, in the darkness of the night,
Enter our own messes, our own darkness,
And bring new life and new hope.
In the name of Emmanuel, God-with-us, Amen.

Suggested Hymns
"Come Thou Long Expected Jesus"; Author: Charles Wesley; Composer: Rowland Hugh Prichard; Harmonizer: Ralph Vaughan Williams

"In the Bleak Midwinter"; Author: Christina Rossetti; Composer: Gustav Holst

"Let All Mortal Flesh Keep Silence"; Author: Gerard Moultrie; Composer: Ralph Vaughan Williams

"Oh Come, Oh Come, Emmanuel"; Author: Latin Prose; Composer: Unknown; Adapter: Thomas Helmore; Arranger John Weaver

# 4

# Child Loss, Miscarriage, Infertility, and Parenthood

LOSING A CHILD, HAVING a stillborn baby, and experiencing a miscarriage are deeply traumatic events for parents and their families. Often these deaths and losses are difficult to talk about and are not addressed in church. Sometimes the loss is private, especially for someone who has experienced a miscarriage. While it is important to respect the privacy of those who do not wish to discuss their loss, the church cannot ignore the grieving parents who have lost their precious children or have had their hopes for children dashed over and over again.

Since there are many layers to parenthood and childhood, this chapter offers a number of resources for the particular types of pain in this area. I offer a worship service for child loss and miscarriage which can be used for Pregnancy and Infancy Loss Awareness Day on October 15. I offer an inclusive litany and prayer for both Mother's and Father's Day, to honor all the complicated emotions and experiences in regards to being and/or having mothers and fathers. I offer prayers to be used in private for those who have experienced a miscarriage, a stillbirth, or are experiencing infertility. May these words provide comfort.

Breath for the Breathless

## WORSHIP SERVICE

*A bouquet of flowers will need to be purchased and placed near the pulpit for the act of remembrance.*

Litany
  Leader: Siblings in Christ, those who have lost a child or a pregnancy,
  **People: We see you, we love you, and we support you.**
  Leader: Your story matters to God who feels your pain.
  **People: Your story matters to us, the church.**
  Leader: We will walk through grief and pain together, relying on the grace of God.
  **People: We will pray for one another and live in the hope of the resurrected Christ.**

Opening Prayer
Merciful God, we enter into this time of worship with heavy hearts. We turn our eyes upon you, knowing that our help comes from you. We offer our whole selves today: our pain, our grief, our anger, all that we are. Please reassure us of your acceptance and grace. Oh God, meet us here today. Amen.

Hymn

Prayer of Illumination
Spirit of the Living God, we know that your word is alive and active. The words we are bombarded with often clutter our minds and weigh us down. Clear out the noise of the words of the world so that we may only hear you. Amen.

Scripture Suggestions and Meditation
*Instead of a sermon or homily, read each Scripture and offer a couple of sentences of reflection. Then pause for a moment of silence and contemplation. This can be done in complete silence, or perhaps bells could chime after each reading, three rings for the Trinity.*
Psalm 38:9–11; Isaiah 11:1–9, 15; Mark 10:13–16; 2 Corinthians 1:3–7

Hymn

Affirmation of Faith (from John 11)
We believe that Jesus, fully God and fully human, deeply loves humankind. Jesus cared for his friends on earth and valued human life. Our Savior was moved to tears when Lazarus died, and he wept with Mary and Martha. Jesus is moved by our pain, and he weeps with us. Christ proclaimed that he is the resurrection and the life. We believe that Jesus is the Messiah, the Son of God, and that those who die in Christ will be raised again, like Lazarus. All honor and praise to our Lord Jesus Christ.

Prayer of the People
God of strength, you are mighty to save. Thank you for holding us when we are weary and taking all of our pain and anger. Sometimes we need a stronghold to shelter us from the storm. Please hold us tight in those times. Sometimes we need to rage, and we need a haven to speak or scream aloud. Please be our safe place when we need it. For each person who has lost a child or has experienced a miscarriage, we pray that you will be their strength.
**Lord, make haste to save us.**
God of gentleness, you surround us with your presence. Thank you for never forsaking us. Sometimes we need comfort and consolation. Please whisper your peace into our hearts when we need to hear a word from you. Sometimes we are not ready for comfort, but we need to know that we're not alone. Please be our companion in those moments. For everyone who has experienced loss here, we pray that you will be a source of gentleness.
**Lord, make haste to save us.**
God of eternal love, you are the God of the past, the present, and the future. Thank you for being with us always. Sometimes we are anxious and worried about the future. Please reassure us that wherever we are, you are there with us. Sometimes the wounds of the past hurt us in the present. Please heal us so that we can move forward. For everyone who aches with grief, we pray that you will encompass them in the love of eternity.
**Lord, make haste to save us.**

The Lord's Prayer

Acts of Remembrance
*A familiar hymn may be played or sung as the congregation is invited to come forward. The pastor or presider will dip their hand in the baptismal font and make a sign of the cross on each person's forehead, speaking a blessing over them. This is a reminder that God has a claim over our lives, even in death. Then the congregant may take a flower from a bouquet at the front of the sanctuary as a remembrance of their lost child or lost pregnancy.*

Blessing
Remember your baptism. Remember that God has claimed you. In life and death, you belong to God. Amen.

Hymn

Benediction (From Philippians 4)
May your gentleness be known to everyone, for the Lord is near.
May the peace of God that passes all understanding
Guard your heart and mind in Christ Jesus.
The grace of the Lord Jesus Christ be with your spirit. Amen.

Suggested Hymns
- "Abide with Me"; Author: Henry Francis Lyte; Composer: William Henry Monk
- "God of Great and God of Small"; Author and Composer: Natalie Sleeth; Arranger: Beverly A. Howard
- "Great is Thy Faithfulness"; Author: Thomas O. Chisholm; Composer: William Marion Runyan
- "Sacred the Body"; Author: Ruth Duck; Composer: Colin Gibson

## MOTHER'S DAY

## Litany

Leader: Today we honor those who have mothering hearts. We honor all mothers:

People: Mothers of little children, mothers of teenagers, mothers of adults, single mothers,

Leader: Adoptive mothers, foster mothers, step-mothers, working mothers, and stay-at-home mothers.

People: We honor grandmothers, great-grandmothers, and many generations of women.

Leader: We honor family members who raised and care for children that they didn't give birth to.

People: We support the women who have the hearts of mothers, but never had children of their own.

Leader: We support the mothers who have experienced the pain of child loss and miscarriage.

People: We support the women who have chosen not to have children. We support those who have lost their mothers, never had a mother, or have had estranged or abusive relationships with their mothers.

Leader: We honor those who show tenderness, nurturing, strength, leadership, and intelligence to their children, and for whom the gendered title "mother" doesn't quite fit.

All: It is this expansive love that reflects God's mothering grace showered upon us.

## Prayer of the people

Dear God, Isaiah says your love nourishes and comforts us as a mother. We lean in close to you today. We are grateful for how you provide for us, watch over us, and show us that we are precious in your sight. Thank you for our cherished earthly mothers who reflect this love that comes from you. Teach us how to show our appreciation for the selflessness that mothers shower over us. Help us to return the love given to us. Mama God, we ask that you embrace those who have not had mothering love shown to them here on earth. Whisper comfort to those who longed to be mother but have been unable, or who have lost their children. Hold the hands of those who have lost their earthly mothers. This day is a sweet celebration for many; please multiply their joy, memories, and laughter. This day holds pain for countless others; please hold them close, listening to their cries, and soothing their pain. In the name of your beloved Son, Christ Jesus. Amen.

## FATHER'S DAY

### Litany

Leader: We are grateful for the fathers in our churches, our communities, and our homes.

**People: We are grateful for fathers of children of all ages, grandfathers, single fathers,**

Leader: Adoptive fathers, foster fathers, step-fathers, working fathers, and stay-at-home fathers.

**People: We are grateful for family members who raised and cared for children that aren't their children by birth.**

Leader: We remember those who have the love of a father and the desire for children but have not had children of their own. We remember the fathers who know the grief of losing a child and miscarriage.

**People: We remember the men who have chosen not to have children. We remember those who have lost their fathers, never had a father, or have had estranged or abusive relationships with their fathers.**

Leader: We are grateful for those who offer guidance, nurturing, support, wisdom, and kindness to their children, and for whom the gendered title "father" doesn't quite fit.

**All: It is this self-giving love that we are given a glimpse of the love of our Heavenly Father.**

CHILD LOSS, MISCARRIAGE, INFERTILITY, AND PARENTHOOD

## Prayer of the people

Heavenly Father, we rejoice that you have dwelling places prepared for us in your house. You invite us to come live with you, gathering us in as one family. We praise you for the earthly fathers who provide a glimpse of your expansive love. Teach us how to return the love that our fathers give to us. For those who celebrate this day, increase the loving bond shared, the stories told. Papa God, many of your children do not know the love of an earthly father. Warm them with your love. Hold a space for those who have longed to become fathers and never had their desire fulfilled. Console the fathers who have lost children. Stand by those who have lost their earthly fathers, and fill the void left by their absence. For those who grieve on this day, pick them up and hold them close so that they might know you will never abandon them. We pray this in the name of your Son who is the way to your heart. Amen.

## INDIVIDUAL PRAYERS

## Prayer for those who have experienced a miscarriage

Oh Lord, we know that we can bring everything to you in prayer. No matter what our circumstances are, you are always listening and never shy away from any burden, grief, or pain that we lay down at your feet. Together with *(name of parents)*, we are baring our broken hearts to you today for a pregnancy that has ended in a miscarriage. Dear God, hear your grieving servants as they come to you with prayers of honest expression and raw emotion. Often this is a tragedy experienced in secret because it is difficult to talk about. But today we share the pain as the loving, compassionate family of faith you have called us to be. As we stand together with *(parents)*, help us to support them through this distressing season. Help us, your church, to hear their cries with empathy when they need someone to listen, to respect their privacy when needed, and to show up when they need a helping hand, a distraction, or a loving presence. Precious Lord, while hope may be shattered now, we ask that over time, with patience and healing hope in the resurrected Christ, that life abundant will be restored to *(parents)*. In the name of Jesus, we ask these things. Amen.

## Prayer for those who have experienced a stillbirth

Merciful God, we cast our cares upon you because you are always ready to receive them. Thank you for hearing us. We come to you today with broken hearts, shattered dreams, and unspeakable grief. We are hurting as *(name of the child, or just "this child" if there is no name chosen)* has left us far too soon. It's not fair. We are confused and angry. We ask that you hold *(the name of the parents)* in the palm of your hand. In your mercy, we ask that you hear their questions, their doubts, their anger, and their grief. These emotions are hard to carry, so please carry the emotions for them as they work through the pain. Merciful God, please surround *(parents)* now. Help us, your church, to support them in any capacity they need. Show us how to bear the pain with them and how to be loving companions on this journey of grief. We ask this in the name of your Son, the rebuilder of hope. Amen.

## Prayer for those who are experiencing infertility

Sweet Jesus, Lamb of God, you are our hope and our help. Thank you for your perpetual grace. You are with us when we wait, when our desires go unfulfilled, and when our hope becomes strained. Lord Jesus, *(parents)* have been waiting for so long for a child to love. They have waited, hoped, and dreamed, and now their hearts grow weary. We ask that you be with them in this season of pain and grief. Give them the strength and courage to make decisions about their future in parenthood. Heal their hearts, minds, and spirits. We know that beauty can come from ashes, even if that means our dreams must adapt during life's ever-changing circumstances. May the love they wish to share be felt by others and be given back to them in abundance. We ask these things in your name, our hope and Redeemer. Amen.

# 5
# LGBTQIA+ Remembrance

THE WORLDWIDE CHURCH IS still struggling to accept and affirm the LGBTQIA+ community. Theological disagreements, church member loss, and denominational splits occur everywhere. If your church wants to support the LGBTQIA+ community and affirm their place in the church of Jesus Christ, then this chapter is for you. This worship service is an opportunity to stand against the sins of hate, discrimination, and prejudice.

One way to honor the LGBTQIA+ community is to speak up against the hate, bullying, and violence directed toward them. People who openly express their love for another person of the same sex or publicly celebrate their gender identity are often at risk of violence or even death. I offer this worship service to honor victims of hate crimes and to recognize and affirm the LGBTQIA+ community. This service can be used for various days and times of LGBTQIA+ remembrance, including Pride Month in June, LGBT History Month in October, Transgender Remembrance Day on November 20, or International Day Against Homophobia, Transphobia, and Biphobia on May 17. May these words provide love.

BREATH FOR THE BREATHLESS

## WORSHIP SERVICE

*Prior to this service, collect a list of names of departed LGBTQIA+ people from your community. Each name will be assigned to a person attending the worship service to be read aloud.*

Call to Worship (from Psalm 31)
> Leader: In you, O Lord, I seek refuge; in your righteousness deliver me.
>
> **People: Rescue me speedily. Be a rock of refuge for me, a strong fortress to save me.**
>
> Leader: Be gracious to me, O Lord, for I am in distress; my eyes, my soul, and my body waste away from grief.
>
> **People: My adversaries scorn me, and they whisper plots to take my life.**
>
> Leader: But I trust you, O Lord! Deliver me from the hand of my enemies and persecutors.
>
> **People: Let the wicked be put to shame. Save me in your steadfast love.**
>
> **All: O how abundant is your goodness! We bless you, O Lord!**

Hymn

Call to Confession
God has created the world and everything in it. God called it all good. We have denied the goodness in creation through our prejudice. Let us confess our sins together.

Confession
**Oh God, you invite, beckon, gather, welcome, and include. Thank you for your steadfast love that always seeks to be in relationship with us. We confess that we do not always want to be in relationship with one another. We, as the church, claim that all are welcome, and we have failed to live up to this claim. When people whose sexual orientations and gender identities we struggle to accept enter our houses of worship, we sometimes turn them away and close the church doors behind them. Forgive us for this exclusion, O**

## LGBTQIA+ Remembrance

Lord. Help us accept, affirm, and welcome your beloved children. We ask this in the name of our redeemer, Jesus Christ. Amen.
*(Silence.)*

Assurance of Pardon
God is faithful to God's good creation, seeking to reconcile all people. Live into hope! Jesus Christ has done a reconciling work, making all things new. In the name of Jesus Christ, we are forgiven. Amen.

Prayer of Illumination
Holy Spirit, we need a good word. Speak so that we may mourn but also have hope. Speak so that we may affirm one another and also take action. Embolden us, empower us, and commission us. Holy Spirit, come. Amen.

Scripture Suggestions
Psalm 139:1–6, 13–16; Isaiah 56:1–8; Luke 6:37–42; Romans 12:9–18

Sermon
*Here a sermon may be offered in reflection of the Scriptures. This is an opportunity to talk about affirmation of the LGBTQIA+ community and how God treasures them for who they are. This is an opportunity to lament the lives lost to hate and to denounce the evils of prejudice and violence.*

Hymn

Affirmation of Faith (from John 14)
We believe that God is our parent, our heavenly Father and divine Mother, who loves us. God will never leave us orphaned or abandoned. God makes a home for all to dwell in. We believe that Jesus is the way, the truth, and the life. Jesus prepares a place for us in God's home and speaks peace into our lives. We believe that the Holy Spirit is our advocate who abides with us. The Spirit speaks the truth and teaches us the way to love one another. We believe in love; we love one another, and we see God's love through Jesus Christ. This is the truth of the Spirit in us.

Prayer of the People
Creator God, you have made a beautiful world with majestic mountains, mighty seas, beautiful foliage, and creatures large and small. Thank you for creating the earth and everything in it. Thank you for creating a diverse people who have a variety of gifts, who have varying gender identities and sexual orientations, who have differing callings in life, and who are all worthy of love. We pray for our entire world, that we all treat it with respect and all people with human dignity.
**Help us to show the love of Christ.**
Loving God, thank you for our nation that we live in. We pray for our leaders and lawmakers. Please give them the wisdom to govern with justice, kindness, compassion, and equality. Lord, hold accountable our leaders who oppress the sick, the poor, the LGBTQIA+ community, immigrants, people of color, women, and all people who are exploited by corrupt power. Help us to speak out for leaders who govern with a righteous heart and speak against those who rule with a hurtful spirit.
**Help us to show the love of Christ.**
Merciful God, thank you for our communities, our places of work, our places of study, our neighbors, our friends, and our family. We ask you to be at work in these communities so that all people are safe, valued, and respected. Please bring an end to bullying, discrimination, and violence. Help us to be peacemakers so that no one is afraid of being targeted for expressing themselves and loving themselves fully.
**Help us to show the love of Christ.**
Gracious God, thank you for our places of worship. In our churches and houses of worship, help us to proclaim the Good News for all who are oppressed, who are in need of shelter, all who need food, all who need healing, and all who need reconciliation. Let our church doors burst open wide to welcome in all who stand on the side of love and justice.
**Help us to show the love of Christ.**
Faithful God, thank you for being with us at all times. For all who are afraid for their safety and well-being when they express their love or gender identity, send peace and protection. For all who

## LGBTQIA+ Remembrance

seek to support and affirm the LGBTQIA+ community, send courage, kindness, empathy, and understanding. For all who have lost loved ones to homophobic or transphobic violence, send comfort and consolation. Help us to be brave, fighting for love, faith, and the well-being of one another.
**Help us to show the love of Christ.**

The Lord's Prayer

Acts of Remembrance
*One by one, each person will come to the front of the church and read a name. The congregation will respond with, "Rest in power, rest in light." Then a handbell will chime as the reader lights a candle on a table at the front near the pulpit.*

Commitment of Faith
As the people of God, we commit to loving our neighbors as ourselves. We commit to loving each other radically and inclusively. We will accept all people who are Lesbian, Gay, Bisexual, Transgender, Queer, Intersex, Asexual, Pansexual, Gender Non-Conforming, Gender Non-Binary, and people of varying sexual orientations, gender identities, and self-expression. We will celebrate the diverse body of Christ, reminding each other that we are beloved and cherished in God's heart and in our community of faith. We denounce the sins of hate, prejudice, discrimination, violence, murder, sexual assault, and all forms of treatment that dehumanize God's children. We will leave this place upholding human dignity and speaking out against injustice. We trust that God will do a mighty work of love in us and in the world through our faith. So be it.

Hymn

Benediction
Leave this place today knowing that God our Parent loves and cherishes you,
Jesus Christ invites the diverse body to honor everything that makes you unique,

And the Holy Spirit has given you special gifts that should be celebrated.
May the Holy Trinity guard us as we seek justice for all people,
Showing the world around us that love is love is love is love. Amen.

Suggested Hymns
- "Blest Be the Tie that Binds"; Author: John Fawcett; Composer: Johann Georg Nägeli; Arranger: Lowell Mason
- "I Want to Walk as a Child of the Light"; Author and Composer: Kathleen Thomerson
- "I Will Come to You (You Are Mine)"; Author and Composer: David Haas
- "Love Divine, All Loves Excelling"; Author: Charles Wesley; Composer: Rowland Hugh Prichard

# 6

# Denouncing Racism

WHITE SUPREMACY RALLIES ARE happening in our neighborhoods, and people openly express their racist opinions. People of color are being arrested, incarcerated, and shot as the justice system continually fails to treat all people fairly. People of color who are not originally from this country are being deported, separated from their families, and displaced by our government. These are life-and-death situations based on the color of a person's skin, and the church has a responsibility to stand firm against hate, prejudice, and discrimination. Pastors who speak out are often reprimanded, but we must have these conversations in our churches and work toward more open, compassionate conversation. It takes time and patience but these efforts can have a large impact.

    A church never knows when their own members might be deported, or when white supremacist groups may target their friends and neighbors. People will turn to the church to see where God is in all of this. I offer this worship service as a way to gather those who are hurting into the church to speak out and denounce racism. This service can be used on a holiday like Martin Luther King, Jr. Day or when a community has been suffering under racism. Communion has been added to this service as an act of reconciliation and equality. May these words provide a path to embrace one another.

Breath for the Breathless

## WORSHIP SERVICE

*Each person will need a candle for the final hymn. As people enter the sanctuary, have candles in baskets for everyone to take one.*

Call to Worship (from Ephesians 4)

> Leader: Oh God, we are gathered here as your diverse people, bearing one another in love.
>
> **People: We are gathered in one place, worshipping one Lord, in one faith, with one baptism.**
>
> Leader: We worship you, Oh God, who is in all and works through all.
>
> **People: We are people of all races who are apostles, prophets, evangelists, teachers, and pastors.**
>
> Leader: We are no longer children, blown by the winds of every doctrine and trickery.
>
> **People: We stand in full stature and maturity in Christ.**
>
> **All: We will promote unity, speak the truth against discrimination in love, and promote growth in the whole body of Christ.**

Hymn

Call to Confession
As we seek to be peacemakers in the world to be a part of God's healing, let us not neglect the healing that needs to occur in our lives. All have sinned and fallen short of the glory of God. Let us model our faith by confessing our own sins so that others may turn to repentance and reconciliation.

Confession
**Holy God, you are the God of all people, all nations, all races, and all languages. Thank you for the richness of diversity. We confess that sometimes we have not treated diversity as a gift, but as a threat. We confess that too often we have dehumanized people of a different skin color from ours or people who speak different languages from us. Too often we have only cared about the well-being of people who look like us. Too often we have seen injustice**

and have remained silent. Forgive us for the sins of racism, prejudice, discrimination, and complacency. Merciful God, you call us to a united family of faith. Free us from the bondage of sin so that we may love each other in equality and dignity. In the name of Christ. Amen.
*(Silence.)*

Assurance of Pardon
Just as God forgives us in Christ, we are called to be forgiving, kind, and tender-hearted to one another. We are freed from sin to do the work of reconciliation. In the name of Jesus Christ, we are forgiven. Amen.

Prayer of Illumination
Oh God, we are listening to hear your word, but there is a risk for those who have ears to hear. Hearing your word means we risk being made uncomfortable, being challenged, being called to action, and being transformed. Please speak Lord, because we are willing to take this risk. Amen.

Scripture Suggestions
Exodus 22:21–24; Psalm 67; John 15:12–17; Galatians 3:23–29

Sermon
*Here a sermon that reflects the Scriptures may be shared. It may be helpful to include themes like the destruction of hierarchies, the need for equality, human dignity, defiance and resistance against injustice, and the transforming power of Christ.*

Hymn

Affirmation of Faith (from Amos 5 and Luke 1)
We believe that God requires us to love each other and live justly. God calls us to seek what is good, to lift up the needy, and to help the poor. We believe that our prayers, our songs, and our worship are only pleasing to God when justice rolls down like waters and when righteousness is like an ever-flowing stream. God is mighty; the corrupt in power will be brought down from their thrones. God is merciful; the hungry will be filled with good food and

truth. **We believe in seeking God's righteousness and truth from generation to generation.**

Prayer of the People
Mother God, you nurture us when we feel like motherless children. You are our home when home feels so far away. Thank you for holding us close and caring for us, body and soul, when this world beats us down. Oh, God, how long? How long must we ache and suffer? How long must our moaning and sighing continue? We lament together as a family of faith. We lament those who've been wounded, arrested, discriminated against, and killed because of the color of their skin.

Hear our cries! **Weep with those who weep.**

We lament the white supremacy that riddles our nation with fear, rage, and sin. We lament the discrimination and murderous intent of those who hate and fear people because of their race. We lament the rallies that pound the streets and echo against our buildings. We lament the vandalism, the hate crimes, and the refusal of service and employment.

Hear our cries! **Mourn with those who mourn.**

We lament the justice system which targets people based on their skin color. We lament unjust phone calls to authorities for crimes not committed, and the unfair questioning, detention, and arrests that often follow. We lament mass incarceration which orders unfair sentences for small crimes, abuses prisoners instead of restoring them, and promotes repeat offenses.

Hear our cries! **Weep with those who weep.**

We lament the complacency of people who believe they are not directly affected by racism. We lament the refusal to learn and improve our words and habits because it requires self-reflection and work. We lament when people steal from other cultures for fashion, music, and art, but continue to ignore and oppress the cultures they have stolen from. We lament when people refuse to speak up against injustice for fear of losing friends, respect, or employment.

Hear our cries! **Mourn with those who mourn.**

Dear God, you have heard our pain, our confession, and our desires. Pour out your Spirit in waves and billows that overwhelm the world with the ever-flowing stream of justice and righteousness. Transform us again and again as people who glorify you and honor your image in all people. Forgive us of our sins, and commission us to be justice-seekers and peacemakers. We ask these things in the name of Jesus, wrongly accused, arrested, executed, and resurrected. Amen.

Invitation to the Table
This is the table of our Lord Jesus Christ, where you belong, where I belong, where we all belong, seated next to each other as equals and friends. At this table we eat of the same bread, drink of the same cup, share in one baptism, and proclaim the life and resurrection of Jesus Christ as one church body. All who believe in the unity of the Body of Christ are invited to come and partake in this holy meal.

Great Thanksgiving
The Lord be with you. **And also with you.**
    Lift up your hearts. **We lift them up to the Lord.**
    Let us give thanks to the Lord our God. **It is right to give our thanks and praise.**
    God of all people and every age, we praise you for your creative love in the world. You have woven together our great story of humankind. Your narrative of welcome, inclusion, and love for one another was established in your covenant with Israel. When you provided the law for your people in the wilderness, you commanded them to welcome strangers with kindness, because they were once strangers. Your prophets proclaimed your message of caring for the widow, the orphan, and the poor. God of the stories of old, your covenant is that of welcome and steadfast love. Therefore, we praise you singing the song of old:
    **Holy, holy, holy Lord, God of power and might, heaven and earth are full of your glory. Hosanna in the highest. Blessed is the one who comes in the name of the Lord. Hosanna in the highest.**
    Oh God, your Son, Jesus Christ, told us to love you with all of our hearts, souls, and minds and to love our neighbors as ourselves. This is the commandment on which the law of the prophets hangs, and this is the new covenant established by Christ.
    *(Words of institution)*

This is the Good News that we are called to love one another, and this is the message that you sent the Holy Spirit to help us share with the entire world. By the power of the Spirit of word and fire, you gave the apostles the ability to speak the message of our Lord and Savior to all people in every tongue. In this inclusive message of the Gospel, we proclaim the great mystery of faith:
**Christ has died, Christ has risen, Christ will come again.**

Bless us with your Holy Spirit and bless these elements of bread and wine so that in partaking of this meal, we participate in your covenantal love of welcome and unity. We come to the table praising your holy name and continuing your divine story written for humankind, proclaiming the life, death, and resurrection of Christ until the New Heaven and New Earth come to bring all pain and suffering to an end. **Amen.**

The Lord's Prayer

Communion

Commitment of Faith
As the Body of Christ, we commit to celebrating the diversity of all people. We believe that God loves people of all ages, races, ethnicities, nations, and languages. We denounce the sin of racism. We believe our differences are our strength. We will fight against the injustice of discrimination and prejudice. We will speak out against white supremacy, murder, violence, and all crimes committed against people of color. We will seek the justice and righteousness of God by holding people accountable for their racist actions, acknowledging our own biases, and continuing to learn and reform. We will love our neighbors as ourselves. So be it.

Hymn and Candle Lighting
*For the final hymn, the song "This Little Light of Mine" can be sung as everyone holds and lights a candle. Ushers can come down the aisles to light the person's candle at the end of the pew, and the light can be passed down to everyone else's candles. This is to represent the light of Christ and is an act to represent peacemaking and resistance to evil.*

Benediction (from 1 Corinthians 16)

## Denouncing Racism

Be alert, stand firm in faith, be courageous and strong.
Let everything you do be done in love.
Greet one another with a holy embrace.
The grace of the Lord Jesus be with you. Amen.

Suggested Hymns
- "For the Troubles and the Sufferings of the World"; Author and Composer: Rodolfo Gaede Neto; Translators: Jorge Lockward, Simei Monteiro; Harmonizer: Jorge Lockward
- "Goodness is Stronger than Evil"; Author: Desmond Tutu; Composer: John L. Bell
- "I'm Gonna Eat at the Welcome Table"; Author and Composer: Traditional African-American Spiritual; Arranger: Carl Dilton
- "This Little Light of Mine"; Author: Traditional African-American Spiritual; Arranger: William Farley Smith
- "We Shall Overcome"; Author: Traditional African-American Spiritual; Arranger: William Farley Smith

# 7

# Closing a Church

CHURCH ATTENDANCE HAS BEEN in decline for years, and more and more congregations have found themselves unable to sustain their ministries. Sometimes this involves revisioning the church with new mission statements, cutting budgets, and trying new evangelism strategies. Other times, this leads to a congregation deciding to close its doors. This is a difficult and painful decision. For the congregations who decide to dissolve and dismiss, it is an emotional loss for the members of the congregation who may feel that they are losing a home and a family. Fear, anger, doubts in faith, deep sadness, and many other emotions may follow. Careful and loving pastoral care rests on the shoulders of the pastoral leader, who is likely mourning as well. Creating the closing worship service may seem like an impossible task, but the last worship service as a congregation is incredibly important for closure for everyone. I offer this template of a worship service to help create a meaningful time of worship for the closing congregation. Communion has been added to this worship service as a reminder to the congregation that they are still one body and one church in Jesus Christ. May these words provide hopeful closure.

CLOSING A CHURCH

## WORSHIP SERVICE

Call to Worship (from Psalm 90)
 Leader: Lord, you are our dwelling place for all generations.
 **People: Before you brought forth the mountains or formed the world, you were everlasting to everlasting.**
 Leader: The years pass and our years end like a sigh.
 **People: Teach us to count our days to make our hearts wise.**
 Leader: Have compassion on your servants; satisfy us with your steadfast love.
 **People: Let us rejoice and be glad all of our days.**
 **All: Let the favor of God be upon us and prosper the work of our hands.**

Hymn

Call to Confession
As the season of this congregation draws to a close and we face the time to part ways, we have an opportunity before us. This is the moment when all of the hard feelings we have harbored over the years can be released to God. Let us lighten our hearts and lay down the burden of grudges and regrets by confessing our sins together.

Confession
**Gracious God, you have blessed our church through the years. Thank you for the memories in this congregation. Where there are friends and family, there will be love, but there will also be conflict. As broken people live life together, our words and deeds will sometimes hurt each other. We confess that we have done hurtful things, held onto grudges, refused forgiveness, and made decisions that we regret. Forgive us, Lord. Help us to right our wrongs, let go of our resentment, and be freed from our regrets. Let our hearts be light as we put old conflicts to rest. We ask these things in the hope of the risen Christ. Amen.**
*(Silence.)*

Assurance of Pardon
In the Spirit of the Lord, there is freedom. By God's glory we are made into the image of glory. We can have confidence in this through Jesus. In the name of Jesus Christ, we are forgiven. Amen.

Prayer of Illumination
Oh Lord, you have never failed to speak to us when we have gathered to worship you. You will not fail to speak to us going forward. Speak to us now, reminding us of your steadfast love which pursues us wherever we go. Amen.

Scripture Suggestions
Psalm 16: 1–3, 7–8; Isaiah 35; Matthew 6:25–34; 1 Corinthians 12:12–26

Sermon or Homily
*A sermon may be offered in reflection of the Scriptures. The pastor or preacher may be feeling pressure to preach the right sermon considering that it will be the last one for this congregation but preaching the hope of the Gospel of Jesus Christ is always a comfort in times of transition and closure.*

A Time of Testimony
*Many people will want to share memories at this time, but perhaps for the sake of time only have two or three people pre-selected to share a story or memory about the church.*

Hymn

Affirmation of Faith (from Isaiah 43)
**We believe that God has created us, formed us, and redeemed us. God has told us that we are loved and precious in God's sight. We believe that when we pass through troubled waters, God will be with us. God has promised that the rivers will not overwhelm us and that the fire will not consume us. We believe that God will deliver us by the work of God's hand, and no one can hinder it. We are the sons, daughters, and children of God who have been formed to glorify God. We will not be afraid.**

## Closing a Church

Prayer of the People
God of the ages, you have been with us in the years past, and we know that you will be with us for years to come. We praise you for all the beautiful, wonderful, and difficult times we've had together as a congregation. Thank you for the laughter and the memories we've shared together. We are grateful for the meals we've had, our Bible studies, the baptisms, the broken bread and poured cup, the Easters and Christmases, the worship, the service to others, and the fellowship. Thank you for our shared experiences and shared tears. We are grateful for our community that has rallied around us during illness, loss, funerals, weddings, births, and all of life's transitions. Oh Lord, thank you for giving us this family of faith. We remember *(here you can add specific memories about the church, such as Vacation Bible School, the Easter egg hunt, the church camp out, etc.)*

    While we smile as we reflect on our lives in this congregation together, we cannot neglect the ache in our hearts as this time comes to a close. God, we know that you are near to the brokenhearted, and we need your comfort now. Be with us as we hold each other close and wipe away each other's tears. These tears are a sign of our love and devotion to you, Oh Lord, and our love for each other. Be with us in the days to come as we go forward and journey through our grief. Console us as we say goodbye to this era. Give us hope and courage as we look forward to the next chapter unfolding before us. While we are stepping out and leaving this congregation for now, reassure us that we are still part of the church of Jesus Christ. We are the church body, and that will continue. This is still our family of faith, and there are more members of the church body who will welcome us into their congregations. We are confident that you will be with us each and every step of the way. Gracious God, we ask for your peace and blessing as we leave this place today. We pray this in the name of Jesus, the Head of the church, and the Lord of our lives. Amen.

Invitation to the Lord's Table
Siblings in Christ, this is Christ's table for the whole church. We can find Christ here, today and always. When institutions close, when relationships are strained, when times are uncertain, this table will

always stand for the Body of Christ. Beloved, you are welcome here. If ever you find yourself lost and confused, know that this table is where you belong. Come, all who are here, to celebrate the Lord's Supper.

Great Thanksgiving
The Lord be with you. **And also with you.**
  Lift up your hearts. **We lift them up to the Lord.**
  Let us give thanks to the Lord our God. **It is right to give our thanks and praise.**

All glory, honor, and praise we give to you, oh God, who is the source of all goodness. You have richly blessed your people with sustenance from the fruits of the garden of Eden, to the manna in the wilderness; from the bread and wine prepared by Lady Wisdom to the bread and wine blessed and given by Christ Jesus. You provide us with food to sustain our souls and living water so that we may never thirst. You fill the hungry with good things, and your grace overflows. Together we join our voices with all the glory of creation to sing:

**Holy, holy, holy Lord, God of power and might, heaven and earth are full of your glory. Hosanna in the highest. Blessed is the one who comes in the name of the Lord. Hosanna in the highest.**

You are holy and mighty, and blessed is your Son, Jesus Christ, the Messiah who resisted the evil and temptation of this world so that he could be our Savior and our Friend. This is the Good News of Jesus Christ that all who are scared, all who are alone, all who are sick, all who are struggling, all who are oppressed, all who are fighting fear and sadness, all who are lost, all who are hungry, all who seek righteousness can find what they need in the Way, the Truth, and the Life. It is by his death and resurrection that we can overcome the grasp of evil and death.

*(Words of institution)*

With grateful hearts and prayerful spirits, we remember the grace given by the sacrifice on the cross and the victory given by Jesus freed from the tomb. Together we proclaim the mystery of faith: **Christ has died, Christ has risen, Christ will come again.**
Send forth your Holy Spirit, rushing into the world, refreshing your people, and blessing these elements of bread and wine. By

this blessing, may we know that in sharing this meal we are forever united in your love. Reassure us that we are claimed by your love and that we belong to you in the name of Christ. All praise to you, God of all creation, now and forever. **Amen.**

The Lord's Prayer

Communion

Hymn

Dismissing Prayer
*At this time the congregation is invited to join hands in a circle.*
Dismiss us now, Oh Lord, to continue loving and serving you in the name of Jesus Christ. Grant us peace, power, courage, and strength to face this ending and this new beginning. We take our memories as we go, and we leave our regrets behind. God, be with us in our coming and our going, now and forever. Amen.

Benediction (from Ephesians 6)
Let the Holy Spirit encourage your hearts,
And give peace to all in this community.
Have faith in God.
Grace is given to all who have an undying love for Jesus Christ.
Go in peace, hope, and love. Amen.

Suggested Hymns
- "God Be with You 'Til We Meet Again"; Author: Jeremiah Eames Rankin; Composer: William G. Tomer; Alternative tune composer: Ralph Vaughan Williams
- "Guide Me, O Thou Great Jehovah"; Author: William Williams; Translators: Peter Williams, William Williams; Composer: John Hughes
- "Lord, Dismiss Us with Your Blessing"; Author (attributed to): John Fawcett; Alterer: Godfrey Thring; Composer: Unknown
- "My Hope is Built on Nothing Less"; Author: Edward Mote; Composer: William Batchelder Bradbury

# 8

# Liturgy for Various Circumstances

## ABUSE

ABUSE HAPPENS IN OUR congregations, right under our noses. Far too often, it goes unseen and unreported because accusations of abuse are frequently dismissed. It happens to people of all gender identities and ages in all types of relationships. LGBTQIA+ survivors often have difficulty finding the help they need because many resources only address heterosexual cisgender couples. Even when the resources are known and readily available, people experiencing abuse may not be ready to leave because it may put them or their children in greater danger. One way to recognize abuse is to admit that it happens in our churches and commit to believing people who say they are being abused. Liturgy is not the answer to abuse but speaking it aloud in our churches can open our eyes and inspire us to be prepared if someone asks for help. The litany and the prayer of the people can be used in worship, specifically during Child Abuse Prevention and Awareness Month in April or Domestic Violence Prevention Month in October. The prayer for someone who has survived abuse can be used in private for an individual seeking pastoral care. I offer this liturgy as an avenue to talk about abuse and arm ourselves with resources. May these words provide hope.

## Litany (From 1 John 4)

Leader: God is love, and if we love one another God lives in us.

**People: God's love is perfected in us, and perfect love casts out fear.**

Leader: Those who say they love God, but hate others speak lies.

**People: Those who say they love someone but abuse them speak lies.**

Leader: Physical, sexual, and emotional abuse do not come from love, but from the evil of sin.

**People: We reject the sin of abuse and commit to caring for the abused.**

**All: Oh God, let your perfect love in us move us to believe, help, and shelter those who are being harmed.**

## Prayer of the people

God our creator, who calls us to be a relational people, you bring life and fellowship. You command us to love each other as we love ourselves. When sin infects our lives, our relationships are broken. Sometimes these broken relationships become dangerous and abusive. We hold these concerns up to you Creator.

**God, heal what is broken.**

Jesus, our wounded savior, you know what it is like to be emotionally and physically abused. You see the people in our world, people of all ages and genders, who have been physically, sexually, emotionally, and psychologically abused. Christ, you have overcome death; please end this evil cycle of abuse. We hold these concerns up to you, our Savior.

**Jesus, heal what is broken.**

Holy Spirit, you are our ever-present advocate. You are at work in the world, compelling our hearts to pursue justice. Open

our hearts to believe those who speak up for themselves or others who experience abuse. Equip us to shelter and protect those who flee abusive situations. We hold these concerns up to you, Advocate. **Holy Spirit, heal what is broken.**
God, three-in-one, you are in the midst of the pain. Empower us to stand up against abuse and listen to and help those who have been abused. Guide those fleeing abuse to safety and send forth healing for their whole being. Pour out your justice on those who harm your children, hold them accountable for their actions, and completely transform their violent ways. In the name of the healing Christ. Amen.

## Prayer for a survivor of abuse

God, our help and our strength, you are mighty to save. Thank you for being our stronghold and refuge. We ask that you pour out your ever-flowing love onto *(name.)* Be their strength and healing as they move forward into hope, and away from the despair that has had a hold on their life. Reassure *(name)* of their worth, value, and purpose in this world and as your beloved child. We, as the church, renounce the evil of abuse and uphold the values of kindness, human dignity, and reconciliation. Help us to support *(name)* with all of our resources and love, listening to and providing for them. We have confidence in your grace through your Son, Jesus Christ, who was abused and overcame. It is in his name we ask these things. Amen.

## ADDICTION

We are learning more about the disease of addiction and how it affects individuals and families. Churches are opening their doors to the gatherings of groups such as Alcoholics Anonymous (AA), Narcotics Anonymous (NA), and Al-Anon which supports families of those affected by addiction. It is important to respect the anonymity of those in attendance, so churches would likely not be involved in these groups by offering worship services. However, the pastor of the church may want to pray a blessing over the room being used

## Liturgy for Various Circumstances

for these groups when no one is around. The pastor could pass this blessing onto the group leader who could then decide whether they would share it with the people in the group.

When addiction claims lives, the family may need the comfort of the church, and for their specific grief and pain to be named. Anonymity should be carefully protected, but speaking aloud the pain of addiction, overdose, and loss, when requested by the family, could bring encouragement to families who need to hear these topics addressed. There are two options for prayers here: individuals and families who are battling addiction together and families who have lost a loved one to addiction. The prayer for individuals and families can be shortened for the individual. These may be offered in private for people and families who are seeking pastoral care. I offer this liturgy as a support to those who wish to encourage and support those fighting addiction and on the road to recovery; these words are also for those who are grieving those they've lost to addiction. May these words provide a safe place.

### Room blessing

Holy Spirit, thank you for abiding with us each day. Let your presence be known as you dwell in this room. Be at work in each person who walks through these doors to create a sanctuary of safety, restoration, and understanding. Hold space for laughter, tears, storytelling, and healing. May the bond of this community break the chains of destruction. In the name of Christ our Redeemer. Amen.

### Prayer for individuals battling addiction and their families

Compassionate God, you know us by name and love us for who we are. You see our victories and celebrate them with us; you see our struggles and you do not turn away from us. You love us entirely and wholly, never leaving us or forsaking us. God our maker, we pray for *(name)* who is battling the disease of addiction. Be with them in the days, weeks, and years to come as they fight to overcome and pursue health and wholeness. Be with *(name)* as they reach out to *(rehabilitation facility, addiction group, medical facility, etc)* for healing. Strengthen *(name)* to fight addiction with help from others and to know their value, worth, and beauty. Empower the *(community leaders, medical workers, professional therapists, etc.)* to care for *(name.)* We are so grateful for *(name)* and all the blessings, gifts, and talents they bring to our community. Help us as the church to be a loving support to them in any way that they need.

Gracious God, please be with *(name's)* family members, *(name of all the family.)* Comfort them in their pain, quell their fears, and provide them with patience and understanding as they stand by *(name.)* Help this family to stand in undivided love and support for one another to seek the help that they all need for healing. Help us as the church to be listening ears and servants to this family with the love of Christ as our hope and guide. God, we ask for your loving guidance and your liberating faithfulness in the name of Jesus Christ. Amen.

## Prayer for families who have lost someone to addiction

Merciful God, you are faithful, and you remember us in our pain. Thank you for hearing us. Lend an ear to us now, heed our sighing and our groaning, because our grief runs deep today. We have lost *(name)* to the disease of addiction. They left us far too soon, and we are in shock and mourning. Oh God, it is so hard for us to understand why this has happened; all we know is that we ache from missing *(name.)* We trust that in life and death we belong to you and that nothing, no powers of this world or even death itself, can separate us from your love. Please Lord, pour your peace and comfort over *(names of family members).* Journey with them through their grief, and bring healing for their hearts. Help us as your church to support them in any capacity that they need. Help us to hold a space for their grief and pain so that they will feel loved by their family of faith. We desperately miss *(name)* and nothing will be able to fill that void. But we trust in your unfailing love to support us in the days, weeks, months, and years to come. We ask these things in the name of Jesus who understands the depths of human despair and provides everlasting life. Amen.

## FAMILY DYNAMICS (ABANDONMENT, ESTRANGEMENT, REJECTION)

Churches are full of families of all different types made through marriage, divorce, adoption, friendships, remarriage, committed relationships, single parenthood, and many other varieties. While some have strong, supportive families that they can count on, others have complicated relationships with their families. When holidays such as Mother's and Father's Day arise, or times of gathering such as Thanksgiving and Christmas, those with complicated family dynamics can feel isolated both by their loved ones and by the church. Some people may struggle with abandonment, some are estranged from their families, and others are rejected by their family for things like sexual orientation, gender identity, a choice that the family disagreed with, or any number of conflicts. I offer this liturgy for those dealing with complicated family dynamics. The litany and prayer of the people can be used in a general worship service or near a holiday when remembering those who feel lonely or abandoned. There is also a prayer to use in private for someone who is estranged from their family and seeking pastoral care. May these words provide support.

## Litany

Leader: Oh God, we are gathered here today, and we honor all who find themselves hurting.

**People: For those who have been abandoned by a loved one or felt abandoned by their family, we see you.**

Leader: For those who have complicated relationships with their family, who are feeling tense and estranged from them, we see you.

People: For those who have been rejected by a family who cannot accept them for who they are, we see you.
Leader: For those who have been cut out of a loved one's life, we see you.
People: We are the body of Christ, and we are your family of faith.
All: We commit to loving you and supporting you, just as God loves you.

## Prayer of the people

God our divine Parent, we are gathered here together as a family of faith. We are grateful that you call us together and for the company we have in each other. As the body of Christ, we have committed to be in relationship with you and with each other. You have commissioned us to love one another, loving our neighbor as ourselves. We belong to one another and have a responsibility to one another. Help us to do the hard of work of loving each other well so that we may honor and glorify your name. Help us to be mindful of this when we enjoy times of celebration and gathering with our earthly families. While we watch other families gather, some of us are hurting because we don't all have that option. Some of us gathered here are feeling abandoned, lonely, and estranged from our families. Oh God, be our comfort. You know exactly how complicated and messy our lives can be, and you know through Jesus Christ what it is like to be abandoned, rejected, and betrayed by loved ones. You have promised never to abandon or forsake us. Help us to do the same for each other. Show us how to be inclusive, to invite people into our lives, and how to rally around all who are lonely and in need of support. In the name of Jesus Christ. Amen.

## Prayer for someone who is estranged from family

Christ Jesus, you are our dearest friend. Thank you for showing us the beauty of loving people, even at the risk of being rejected. Jesus, you know what rejection, abandonment, and betrayal from your

## LITURGY FOR VARIOUS CIRCUMSTANCES

closest friends and family feel like. This is a pain that cuts deep into the soul, and you were willing to come and suffer under this pain to show the whole world your love. As someone who understands this pain, I ask that you come and shower your grace upon *(name.)* Your child is hurting and is in need of a friend. The pain they are feeling of being rejected is unfair and unloving. They need a Savior who knows and understands where they are, who they are, and what they are going through. Surround *(name)* with the peace and love they need at this moment. Help us, your church, do our part to be their family of faith in this time of need. Show us how to be a community that tends to one another's needs and cares for one another. We ask all of these things in things in your name. Amen.

## PERIODS OF ILLNESS

Cancer affects everyone's lives, whether we suffer from it directly or our loved ones are being treated for it. Many other chronic diseases such as Rheumatoid Arthritis, Multiple Sclerosis, Alzheimer's, and other illnesses attack the body and the brain and grow worse over time. Some individuals are continually sick or undergo multiple surgeries, without a known or singular cause. Constant physical illness can also debilitate an individual's mental and spiritual well-being. I offer these prayers for private visits for those with chronic illnesses and their caregivers. May these words provide healing.

### Prayer for chronic illness

Precious Lord, you will never leave or forsake us. Thank you for your eternal and steadfast love. Oh God, when illness strikes we are left with many emotions: fear, confusion, anger, and sadness. Breathe your breath of life on *(name.)* Sing a song of peace and comfort over them, so that they may be assured that they can lean into your strong and nurturing arms. Walk with *(name)* as a companion when facing every battle, and carry them when they need to rest. Bless the work of the hands of the doctors, nurses, and caregivers who tend *(name's)* needs. We ask this in the name of Jesus Christ, who is the Healer and Victor. Amen.

## Prayer for Dementia, Alzheimer's, and those who have difficulty communicating

God our Good Shepherd, you are eternal and unchanging. We can rest assured in your never-failing grace. When our daily reality shifts and changes and we are unable to be present or express ourselves in the ways that we wish we could, please be our peace and our comfort. Oh God, be a reassuring presence for *(name)* during times of frustration, confusion, and uncertainty. Be their ever-present help, showing your tender, loving care. Ease their spirit and bless them with your comfort. We ask these things in the name of your Son, Jesus Christ. Amen.

## Prayer for caregivers, nurses, and doctors

Jesus who ministered through healing, thank you for showing us the value of human life, health, and well-being. In your tender mercy, we ask that you bless *(name)* with confidence, peace, wisdom, and compassion for all they provide care for. Let their skills and expertise bless those in need of a healing touch. Work through *(name)* as they answer the calling to the vocation of care and healing. Grant them strength and comfort when their work provides challenges and complications, when illness seems relentless, when death comes for those they care for, and when they provide care for a grieving family. May we all remain thankful for the gift of your presence, Lord Jesus, through the journey of healing and compassion. In your name, amen.

## WHEN A PERIOD OF MINISTRY COMES TO AN END

When a minister comes to the end of a time of service, it can be an emotional period. Whether a pastor is moving to another ministry

## Liturgy for Various Circumstances

or retiring, the time is both sad and joyful. There are two prayers, one prayer for appreciation of a pastor who is leaving and one for a pastor who is retiring. In both cases, it is appropriate to have another church leader like an elder or deacon to say the prayer.

There is also a prayer for a pastor who has been forced out of their ministry. Termination of any kind is deeply painful for the minister and the congregation. Sometimes it is a necessity for the church and for the minister; other times it is a final blow after a long period of toxicity and abuse. Sometimes it is seen coming; other times it comes out of the blue. A trusted colleague or supportive group can pray this prayer to strengthen the individual in this difficult time. I offer these prayers for transitioning pastors. May these words offer appreciation and reassurance.

### Prayer for appreciation of a pastor

Faithful God, you call your people to love and serve you. We give you thanks and praise for those you have gifted and called to ordained ministry. Today we give thanks for the ministry of *(honorific and name)*. They have selflessly given their time, talents, love, leadership, and service to the well-being of our church and to the work of the Gospel. We share our gratitude for the work you have done through them and all the ways our church has been blessed by them. We appreciate the sacrifices they have made, some of which we may never know about. Thank you for the gift of our wonderful minister. While we rejoice in the continuation of their ministry, we also mourn their departure. Gracious God, we ask that you give *(name)* peace, strength, and wisdom as they transition into their next ministry. Please bless the work of their hands as they continue to do the work commissioned by Jesus Christ. We ask this in your Son's name. Amen.

### Prayer for retirement

Eternal God, you are faithful from generation to generation. We praise you for calling us to your service and for our leaders who encourage us in our spiritual vocation. We give you thanks for the leadership of *(honorific and name)* and the years of service they have lovingly provided your church. We give thanks for your Holy Spirit working through *(name)* in every sermon, every prayer, every sacrament celebrated, every hospital visitation, every funeral presided, and every wedding conducted. Oh God, your good and faithful servant has done well. Grant them the rest and relaxation that comes with retirement. Help them find joy in their interests and pursuits as they use this season to be at peace. Reassure *(name)* that they have spent their years serving you and loving your people well. The work that their hands have done will continue to bless the church for years to come. Gracious God, embrace *(name)* in this transition as they navigate what comes next in pursuing their Christian vocation. Provide peace, comfort, confidence, and clarity. Bless them with the knowledge that they still belong to you and the church universal in community and love. We give you praise and ask these things in the name of Jesus Christ. Amen.

## Prayer for a pastor who has been forced out of a ministry

Oh Lord our God, you have called your faithful servant for such a time as this. Thank you for giving *(name)* many talents and gifts for the vocation of ministry. While the call to ministry is a beautiful and exciting challenge, it can also be where we are wounded most deeply. In this painful time, *(name)* needs your blessed reassurance that they are called and claimed by you, and nothing will ever change that. Gracious God, in this transitional season when pain, anger, confusion, and sadness run deep, be a presence of peace. Provide for *(name)* in this uncertain time, help them not to be discouraged in their call, and help them not to doubt the gifts you've given. Surround *(name)* with people who will listen to their hurts and will support them as they search and wait for the next step in ministry. Merciful God, help us have open ears for *(name)* to express uncertainty and frustration. Help us all to have hope together in the church of Jesus and to continue to pursue the great commission of Christ. In the name of your Son, our hope and Redeemer, amen.

# 9

# Praying with Youth

**TRAUMA LESSON PLAN**

**Goal:** Teenagers, like people of any age, have many mixed emotions when trauma happens, and they need the freedom to explore and express themselves. This lesson provides a time and place to process all their complicated feelings.

**Objectives:** The youth will be able to:

- Speak their painful emotions and concerns
- Engage in Bible stories to help them navigate the trauma
- Openly discuss and question their beliefs
- Spend time in reflection on what they have learned
- Channel their pain into positive action
- Create a prayer together and openly speak aloud their concerns

**Method:** The gathering activity uses writing and contemplation to begin to access what the youth are experiencing in the moment. Writing down their painful feelings and experiences on small strips of paper and writing down their hopes on strips of paper to make a prayer chain gives them privacy, which may help them to open up later. Engaging a relevant Bible lesson can help the youth frame their trauma with faith. Including discussion questions helps the youth reflect on the Scripture and provides a space for honest communication. The reflection activities involve critical thinking to produce a positive outcome so that the youth can see that despair can be overcome by hope. The closing prayer is a time for youth to use their voices to proclaim their own needs, concerns, and hopes to God. This shows the support of the faith community and the belief that God hears our prayers.

**Resources:** You will need a few volunteers for facilitation and emotional support. For all of the activities you will need:

- Small strips of paper, six per person
- Clear tape
- Writing utensils such as pens or pencils
- A trash can
- Bibles for the students to read from
- Sheets of paper, one for each student
- Copies of the "Action Plan" form, one for each student

## Gathering Activity

As the students enter, give them each six strips of paper and a writing utensil. Tell them to write down three things that are impacting them negatively. This could be the emotions they are feeling, the trauma(s) that have transpired in the week, something hurtful someone has said or done, etc. Once they have finished, have everyone gather around a trash can. Let the students know that it's okay to feel pain and hurt, but healing can come if we are willing to work through what we are experiencing. This is an opportunity to talk about prayer, community, therapy, and all of the available support to help the youth navigate their pain. Have the youth rip up the negative sheets of paper and throw them away as a symbol of healing. Then have the youth fill in the remaining three strips of paper with prayers and hopes for the future. As they finish, tape all the strips together into a paper chain. This will be a "prayer chain" and will be displayed in the youth room as a reminder of what they are praying and hoping for.

## Bible Lesson

Choose one of the two Bible passages below to read and discuss. The suggested lesson can be used or adjusted to fit the needs of the youth group. The discussion questions are to promote open discussion. Sometimes youth are not willing to share, and this may bring shrugs and silence. Other times, youth just need to know they are allowed to say what's on their mind without fear of judgment. These questions might bring hard questions, strong emotions, and harsh statements. Any of these reactions will need love and support from the adult volunteers as they navigate their faith and their complicated reactions to trauma. It's okay if there are no perfect answers and responses to these questions and doubts. The purpose of these Bible lessons is more to hold a safe place for youth to express themselves and less about teaching them the "right" way to have faith in times of trouble.

## *Option A*

**Topic:** Being honest like Job

**Scripture:** Job 6:1–13; 23:1–17

**Lesson:** Job was a wealthy man with a large family. He was very faithful to God. The heavenly beings, including Satan who was known as the Accuser, were curious if Job would actually be faithful if all of his blessings were taken away. So, Job's children were killed, he lost all of his property and livestock, and he was covered in sores. When all of Job's possessions and family were taken away, he ripped his clothes and shaved his head, but he never sinned. Instead he fell down and worshipped God. His friends came by and tried to comfort him, but they blamed him for his own suffering. They believed Job had been sinful and now he was being punished. Job defended himself; and Job said some very audacious things about God. They were very shocking things to hear from such a righteous man. Job was able to bring his pain honestly before God. At the end of the story, God shows up and tells Job that he doesn't have all of God's wisdom, so he can't possibly understand what God does in the world. However, God does say that Job spoke what was right. God approved of Job's honesty and raw emotions. Job was allowed to express his pain and anger without holding anything back.

Like Job, we don't always have the wisdom to understand why bad things happen or how God is working in the world. But we are allowed to be honest with God about our feelings, doubts, and questions. God understands our pain, and we don't have to hold back. God will hear us when we express ourselves, and this can help lead to healing.

**Discussion questions:**

- How are you feeling?
- Who can you trust to listen or help in times of trouble?
- If you could ask God anything, or tell God anything, what would you say?
- How do you think God feels about pain and suffering?
- How do you think God helps people?
- What is one good thing we can do today to make things a little brighter?

## *Option B*

**Topic:** The diverse Body of Christ

**Scripture:** 1 Corinthians 12:12–31

**Lesson:** A popular metaphor for the church is "the Body of Christ." A body has different members: hands, feet, eyes, nose, fingers, toes, ears, tongue, knees, elbows. Each member of the body serves distinct, important functions. While each member of the body is different, they are all still part of one body. The church is the same way. Each person is different and has an important function. People with various skin colors, people from numerous countries, people who speak different languages, people with various sexual orientations and gender identities are important to God and to the church of Jesus. Everyone brings talents, perspectives, strengths, and weaknesses to the church. All of them are important and unique.

As the body of Christ, we all need each other. We will not function as the body if we say we don't need each other. Prejudices, stereotypes, and discrimination all threaten the body of Christ. If we find ourselves judging people based on their skin color, sexual orientation, immigration status, or political affiliation, it's important to take a step back and address why we feel that way and how we can respond in a compassionate way. If we choose compassion, then we can function as the church better and we are honoring Jesus.

It's also important to love ourselves. God made us unique with gifts and talents specific to us as individuals. We need to know our own value and worth. We are important to God and to the church. We belong here, and we can contribute as functioning members of the body. If we love each other and love ourselves, if we become more accepting and less judgmental, then the body of Christ will become stronger.

**Discussion questions:**

- What are you passionate about?
- What are some of your strengths? Weaknesses?
- What makes you who you are?
- How does it make you feel to be rejected or targeted?
- How can we respect our differences?
- How can we celebrate diversity?
- What does a peaceful world, like the Kingdom of God, look like?

## Reflection Activity

These activities are designed to channel the energy of the group into something positive. While trouble may be occurring on a large scale, these activities can help youth do something good in the world on a small scale. These activities are a reminder that the youth are still part of the Body of Christ, and no matter how bad the world gets they are still a part of Christ's mission in the world.

### Option A

**Affirmation paper:** When there is discrimination and division in the world, it is important for the church to combat prejudice and celebrate diversity. This activity is to help youth affirm one another and feel affirmed by their peers. Provide each student a sheet of paper and a writing utensil. Each student should write their name on top of the sheet of paper. Then everyone will go to a neighbor's paper and write something they admire or appreciate about the person. Everyone will write on each other's papers. Make sure to monitor what's being written just in case someone is tempted to write something hurtful or inappropriate. When it's all finished, give everyone a moment to read over their papers. Ask if anyone would like to share an affirmation that touched them or surprised them. Then challenge everyone to take a moment to write something they like about themselves down on their paper. Encourage them in this, because some may find this to be a difficult task due to low self-esteem. Let them all know that this is how God created them, and God loves all these aspects of each person's character as well. It is a way to celebrate who God created each youth to be and for the community of the youth group to celebrate diversity.

### Option B

**Action plan:** Students will fill out this form to take tangible steps to care for themselves and others during difficult seasons. These are small, easy steps for anyone to take. Even if they can't fill out the whole form, just filling in one or two lines can help youth take positive steps toward healing. The activity is not focused on having the "right" answers but taking positive steps out of negative situations.

## MY ACTION PLAN

I will commit to doing one kind thing for myself this week *(i.e. take a bubble bath, eat a special treat, see a movie, etc.)*
_____
_____.

I will commit to doing one kind thing for another person this week *(i.e. listen to them, give them a ride, invite them over to dinner, help with their homework, etc.)*
_____
_____.

I will commit to helping my family this week *(i.e. taking care of my younger siblings, helping with extra chores, doing things without being asked, etc.)*
_____
_____.

I will commit to praying this week *(i.e. for my neighbors, for my community, for my school, for my friends, etc.)*
_____
_____.

I will commit to making change in the world this week *(i.e. I will contact my government officials, I will volunteer my time, I will donate my allowance, etc.)*
_____
_____.

I will commit to having hope this week *(i.e. hope for recovery, hope for healing, hope for peace, etc.)*
_____
_____.

Breath for the Breathless

## Closing Prayer

This will be an interactive prayer that allows the youth to speak aloud their specific concerns. Some youth may be eager to speak aloud their prayer concerns, or maybe no one will speak up. Regardless of the level of spoken participation, this prayer provides an opportunity for youth to speak to God out loud or silently in their hearts. The youth director or one of the volunteers can read the prayer out loud. Explain to the youth that when the time comes for a pause in the prayer, they can speak aloud their own concerns, or if they feel uncomfortable speaking up, they can silently pray their own prayers. When the pause of the prayer ends, the leader will say, "Lord in your mercy," and everyone else will respond with, "hear our prayer." The prayer will conclude with everyone praying the Lord's Prayer.

Dear God, we bring our heavy hearts to you today because of *(name trauma or tragedy.)* We are overwhelmed with pain, confusion, doubts, and questions. Thank you for hearing us when we need to pray, vent, yell, or cry. Right now, we pray for our communities that we are part of. Each day we go home, go to school, go to the grocery store, the dentist, the doctor, we take our pets to the park, and go to many places in our community. We now name all of parts of the community that need your help:

*(Pause the prayer. Here students can say aloud places like "my school," "my neighborhood," "my house," etc.)*

Lord in your mercy, **hear our prayer.**

Gracious God, your people are hurting right now. *(Take a moment to address the tragedy or trauma and how it has affected the people we love.)* Lord, we seek your love and your help for our friends and family. We watch how the people in our lives are affected by the suffering around them. It hurts us to see our loved ones hurting. We want to help, so we listen, and we pray. We now name all of the people we love who need your help.

*(Pause. Here students can speak up to say, "my mom," "my grandparents," "my friend," etc.)*

Lord in your mercy, **hear our prayer.**

Creator God, we cannot neglect ourselves. We need you too. We hurt, we grieve, we question. We all experience the world differently, so our needs are different. Sometimes we carry anger, sometimes we are looking for answers, sometimes we just want to feel safe. We know that you have created us, and you love us. Please hear us now as we speak aloud the things we need from you.

*(Pause. Here students may say, "help me understand," "peace of mind," "forgiveness," etc.)*

Lord in your mercy, **hear our prayer.**

We ask all of these things in the name of your Son, Jesus, who taught us to pray saying . . . *(The Lord's Prayer)* . . . **Amen.**

# 10

# Praying with Children

### TRAUMA LESSON PLAN

**Goal:** Children need a place to feel safe when times are uncertain. This lesson provides a safe place for children to express how they feel in response to trauma facilitated and framed by faith.

Objectives: The children will be able to:

- Articulate how they are feeling through prayer
- Engage in scripture using their bodies
- Express complicated emotions through art
- Be heard, validated, and attended to by adult volunteers in the church

**Method:** Scripture and movement will be used together to help children embody and engage teachings about faith. The children will put movement to a Bible verse to help them remember the Scripture. Art will help express emotions and perspectives that might be difficult to articulate. Interactive Bible stories and passages will engage the children and help them grasp a faithful understanding of God and tragedies. The fill-in-the-blank prayer is an opportunity for adults to work one-on-one with the children to ask about their emotions and questions regarding the trauma. They can work through the prayer together and once it is completed the child and the adult can pray the prayer.

**Resources:** For this lesson, you will need multiple volunteers so the children can have one-on-one time with adults. You also will need:

- Crayons or markers
- Pens or pencils
- Two sheets of paper for each student
- Strips of colored paper, nine per student; Each strip will have a phrase on it: "food and water," "makes me feel better," "shows me what's right," "I won't be afraid," "comforts me," "makes peace," "goodness," "mercy," and "live with God"
- Glue sticks
- A copy of the interactive story
- Copies of the prayer for each of the children

## Gathering Activity

Once all the children have gathered together, have them stand together, and explain that they are learning a memory verse from the Bible. The memory verse is to help them remember that God is with them even when scary or sad things happen. Explain that you are going to be adding movements to these verses so that it helps them remember them better. They can use these movements and Scriptures to remind themselves of God's love even when they aren't at church. Whenever they are sad, scared, lonely, or confused, they can practice these movements whenever they need them. You can choose from one of the two below:

### Option A

Isaiah 43: 2, "When you pass through the waters, I will be with you."
"When you pass through the waters . . ."
Lean forward, bending one knee as if against a strong current, then move arms in a swimming motion.
" . . . I will be with you."
Stand up straight and wrap yourself in a hug.

### Option B

Psalm 136:1, "Oh give thanks to the Lord, for God is good, for God's steadfast love endures forever."
"Oh give thanks to the Lord . . ."
Raise your hands up towards the heavens and out.
" . . . for God is good"
Bring hands together over your head and clasp them.
" . . . for God's steadfast love endures forever."
Bring clasped hands down over your heart; fold hands, one over the other, over your heart.

## Focus Activity

This is the opportunity to address what has happened to the community: a hurricane, a white supremacy rally, a school shooting, etc. Once everyone has been seated, take a moment to address the event, and then tell the children you want to hear from them what happened and how they are feeling. Ask them to draw a picture of what happened this week in their own eyes. Pass out paper and coloring materials and give them about fifteen minutes to work on their drawing. Volunteers should sit with the children and ask them about their drawings. Here volunteers can ask about specific details, ask to have the children describe the scene, and ask how they are feeling. This gives the child an opportunity to share and tell the story in their own words.

PRAYING WITH CHILDREN

# Bible Lesson

## *Option A*

In these stories about Jesus calming the storm and walking on water, the children can learn about how Jesus helps people face scary events. The children will be part of the story by adding words, reactions, and sound effects. This brings the story to life and makes the Scriptures exciting and understandable. Whatever the kids are facing, they learn that Jesus is with us when bad things happen and sends help from other people.

### JESUS CALMS THE STORM AND WALKS ON WATER FROM MARK 4 AND MATTHEW 14

Jesus was a busy man, teaching, healing, and helping other people. He began attracting large crowds in need of help. The crowds had been following Jesus all day to listen to his teaching *(Everyone cheer "Je-sus! Je-sus! Je-sus!")* And Jesus was tired *(everyone yawns loudly)* so he decided to get away for a little while. Jesus and the twelve disciples got into a boat *(all make loud creaking noises)* to sail away from the crowds. Jesus was so tired that he fell sound asleep *(all make snoring noises.)* Suddenly a huge storm rolled in *(everyone makes loud thunder and rain sounds)* and the waves began getting higher and higher, spilling into the boat! *(All make loud splashing sounds.)* The disciples were so afraid! *(Ahhhhhh!)* They began yelling, "Teacher, teacher wake up!" *(All together, "Teacher, teacher wake up!")* Jesus woke up and said to the wind and the waves, "Peace! Be still!" *(Shhhhhhhh.)* Jesus asked, "Why were you afraid? Don't you have any faith?" *(Uh-oh.)* The disciples were in awe *(everyone covers their mouths and gasps)* and they asked one another, "Who is this that the wind and sea obey him?" *(Wooooow!)*

Then there was another time when Jesus wanted to pray alone. The disciples had been waiting in a boat *(creaking noises)* but waves *(splashing)* and wind *(whoooossssh)* had pushed the boat out to sea. So, Jesus stepped out and began to walk on the water to go to the disciples *(everyone gently clap their hands on their laps *left-right-left-right).* When the disciples saw Jesus walking on the water they thought he was a ghost *(moaning, groaning, and ghost noises)* and they were very afraid! *(Ahhhhhhh!)* Jesus said, "It's me! Don't be afraid!" One of the disciples, Peter, got out of the boat to go see Jesus, and he began walking on the water *(clapping on lap, left-right-left-right.)* But when Peter noticed the strong wind *(whoooosssh)* he became afraid and began sinking! He cried out, "Lord, save me!" *(Everyone yells, "Help me! Help me!")* Jesus reached out, caught him by his hand, and said, "You of little faith, why did you doubt?" *(Uh-oh.)* When they got back into the boat the wind stopped. *(Shhhhhhh.)* And the disciples in the boat worshipped Jesus, saying, "Truly you are the Son of God!" *(Altogether say, "Praise the Lord!")*

Jesus had to face some scary things, but he was able to calm the storms and save his disciples from harm. When we are facing scary things, Jesus sends other people to take care of us. Jesus sends friends, family members, and community members like firefighters, police officers, and doctors to help us. Whatever we are facing, we can trust in Jesus to help us and take care of us.

## *Option B*

This is a call-and-response Bible lesson with some crafting. This will help the children engage with the poetry of this Psalm. Psalm 23 is a passage most children will be taught at some point, and a familiar, comforting Bible passage can create a sense of order and understanding. Give each child nine strips of colored paper with the phrases printed on them. Give each child a piece of paper that says, "The Lord is My Shepherd" on top and a glue stick. Tell the kids to listen to the Psalm closely. Anytime you say, "The Lord is my Shepherd" they will respond with, "God is all I want." Tell them throughout the Psalm there will be keywords to listen for and they will add these keywords to their piece of paper. This piece of paper will help all the children remember what it means for God to be a shepherd and how God provides for our needs.

Psalm 23
The Lord is my Shepherd, **God is all I want!**
A shepherd leads sheep to green pastures, where they can rest, and they have plenty of grass to eat. A shepherd leads sheep to still waters where they have all they need to drink! God is like our shepherd because God gives us everything we need, like food and water. Keywords!

*(Help all the children paste "food and water" to their paper.)*
The Lord is my Shepherd, **God is all I want!**
God restores our souls. Our souls are who we are, all the things that make us happy, all the interests we have, all of our emotions and feelings, and everything that makes us special. God makes our souls feel better. Keywords!

*(Paste "makes me feel better" to papers.)*
The Lord is my Shepherd, **God is all I want!**
God leads us to the right path. God is love, and the way of love is the right way to live. We can trust God to do what is right. Keywords!

*(Paste "shows me what's right" to paper.)*
The Lord is my Shepherd, **God is all I want!**
Even when I walk through the valley of darkness, which means when life gets scary, we won't be afraid! God is always with us, comforting us. Comfort means God is taking care of us. Keywords!

*(Paste "I won't be afraid" and "comforts me" to the paper.)*
The Lord is my Shepherd, **God is all I want!**
God prepares a table for us, even our enemies. This means God loves everyone and includes all people in God's love. Even people who hurt us, God loves. That means God can make peace with all people! When we are with God, there is no more fighting, and we are so grateful for this gift that our love for God overflows. Keywords!

*(Paste "makes peace" on the paper.)*
The Lord is my Shepherd, **God is all I want!**
Surely goodness and mercy will follow the rest of our lives. God will show us how to be good and will be good to us! And mercy means that God will be kind and listen to us, and God will help us when we are in trouble. Keywords!

*(Paste "goodness" and "mercy" on the paper.)*
The Lord is my Shepherd, **God is all I want!**
We will dwell, or live, in God's house for all our lives, forever and ever! Keywords!
*(Paste "live with God" on the paper.)*
Shepherds watch over sheep and protect them. They give them food and water. They show them the right paths to take. God is like a shepherd who watches over us, provides for us, and shows us the right way to live our lives. God shows us goodness, mercy, and peace. And we get to live with God forever. We now have this piece of paper to show us how God is like our shepherd, and we can rely on God in times of trouble. The Lord is my Shepherd, **God is all I want!**

## Closing Prayer Activity

The children and the volunteers pair up to complete this task. Pass out pens and copies of this prayer. The volunteer will go slowly through the prayer and fill it in for the child. They will ask how they are feeling and why they feel that way. They will ask them what they want to ask God to help with or who they want God to help. And then they will ask what the child wants help with for themselves. The volunteer will ask the child if they believe God is bigger than the trauma that has occurred. If the children have trouble answering at any point, or if they have hard questions, or if they become emotional there should be space for this. This activity is less about having the right answers to the prayer and more about asking questions and allowing the children to express themselves. This is an opportunity for support, care, and validation. If the prayer is not completed, the volunteer can still say a short prayer for the child.

Dear God, it's me, *(name)*
_____.

Something big has happened and I am feeling *(sad, scared, confused, etc.)*
_____.

I am feeling this way because *(I lost my favorite toys, my sister is gone, I miss my house, etc.)*
_____
_____.

Please help *(my mom/dad/parent, my friends, everyone, etc.)*
_____.

Please help me *(be brave, be safe, feel better, etc.)*
_____.

God, you are bigger than *(a hurricane, people who hurt other people, all the problems in the world, etc.)*
_____
_____.

Thank you for loving me. In Jesus' name, amen.

www.ingramcontent.com/pod-product-compliance
Lightning Source LLC
Chambersburg PA
CBHW051702090426
**42736CB00013B/2502**